And Then I Gave Up
Essays About Faith and Spiritual Crisis in Islam

~

Umm Zakiyyah

And Then I Gave Up: Essays About Faith and Spiritual Crisis in Islam
By Umm Zakiyyah

Copyright © 2010 thru 2017 by Al-Walaa Publications.
All Rights Reserved.

ISBN: 978-1-942985-11-2
Library of Congress Control Number: 2017904292

Order information at ummzakiyyah.com/store

Verses from Qur'an adapted from Saheeh International, Darussalam, and Yusuf Ali translations.

Published by Al-Walaa Publications
Camp Springs, Maryland USA

TABLE OF CONTENTS

Author's Note	4
Glossary of Arabic Terms	5
PART I: When You Feel Like Giving Up	8
1. And Then I Gave Up: The Ramadan My Brother Died	9
2. 'But I Don't Want Forgiveness'	14
3. Got a Survival Kit? Help for Muslim Apostates	17
4. 'But I Don't Trust God'	21
5. Reality of Ramadan: You Might Not Benefit	24
6. Strawberry Prayers: A Lesson of Ramadan Love	27
7. Walking Wounded: Umm Zakiyyah & Na'ima B. Robert Discuss Spiritual Crisis	30
PART II: Hope for the Confused and Sinful	35
8. Aim High By Aiming Low: Setting Realistic Minimums Instead of Lofty Goals	36
9. I'm Muslim and Don't Pray, What Should I Do?	40
10. Be Careful What You Feed Your Soul	50
11. Is It a Test or a Punishment?	52
12. It's About Your Heart Wants Most	53
13. Good Muslims Do Bad Things Too	55
14. Judgment of Others Is Your Mirror	59
15. Yesterday, I Cried	63
16. He Prayed In a Club!	66

Author's Note

I named the book *And Then I Gave Up* because this particular story, which I share first, summarizes the lessons of faith that I've learned thus far in life, particularly when I felt like I was going to give up on myself and my Lord. I think many of us know how it feels to reach the point where there seems to be no silver lining for our souls. Thus, it is my prayer that the essays in this book serve as a reminder to all believers that no matter what your individual faults and struggles may be, there is always hope—so long as you hold on to our faith, even when you can no longer detect it in your heart.

Umm Zakiyyah
March 2017

Glossary of Arabic Terms

Allah: God
Ameen: Amen
ayah: excerpt of Qur'an or sign from God
bi'idhnillah (or *bi'idhnillaah*): with the help of God
dhikr: remembrance of God
du'aa: prayerful supplication
emaan (or *iman*): faith or sincere belief
halal (or *halaal*): permissible
haram (or *haraam*): forbidden
iftaar: the breaking of fast at sunset
Ishaa: the last of the five obligatory daily prayers
Jannah: Paradise
JazakAllahu khairan: may God reward you with good (an expression of thanks)
Jumu'ah: formal Friday prayer and sermon
inshaaAllah: God-willing
maashaAllah: It was God's will
noor: light or spiritual enlightenment
Qiblah: the direction of Makkah that Muslims face during formal prayer
Salaah: formal prayer
saheeh: authentic
sallallaahu'alayhi wa sallam: may peace and blessing be upon him
shirk: paganism, associating partners with God, or assigning divine attributes to creation
subhaanAllah (or *subhanAllah*): an expression of glorification of God, often said in surprise or deep reflection
Tahajjud: the voluntary night prayer prayed after *Ishaa'* and before *Fajr*
Tarawih: another name for *Tahajjud*
Tawheed: Oneness of God as defined by Islamic monotheism
Witr: the voluntary odd unit(s) of prayer offered at the end of *Tahajjud*
zakaah: obligatory charity paid from the Muslim's wealth

For those who refuse to give up on themselves, or their Lord.

"If something is troubling you to the point of anxiety and frustration because you have no idea how things will end up, then look to three things: your heart, your tongue, and your hands. If your heart is repentant and patient, if your tongue is uttering prayers of forgiveness and God's praise, and if your hands are busy with good, then receive glad tidings, bi'idhnillah. *For your Lord says, "Is there any reward for good except good?" But if your heart is restless and impatient, if your tongue is uttering angry outbursts and complaints, and if your hands are busy with sin, then woe to you. You should stop and repent—and still receive glad tidings, for your Lord says,*
'I am All-Forgiving, Most Merciful.'"
—excerpt of *FAITH. From the Journal of Umm Zakiyyah*

PART I
When You Feel Like Giving Up

Giving up is worse than sin.
Sinning can inspire repentance, but giving up can inspire disbelief.
And God forgives sins, not disbelief.
So don't despair.
Repent.

—excerpt of *Broken Yet Faithful.*
From the Journal of Umm Zakiyyah

1

And Then I Gave Up
The Ramadan My Brother Died

♦

Oh, I had so many high hopes that Ramadan. My schedule included completing my Qur'anic reading in English and supplementing it in Arabic. I was going to memorize a new chapter of Qur'an and read an Islamic book every week. I was going to listen to an Islamic lecture CD each day, and I even scheduled an "Islamic class" with my daughter for every Friday.

O Allah! I prayed. *Put* noor *in my heart and on my face, and make me amongst those whom when people see them, they are reminded of You!*

This particular supplication was inspired by my having recently read about the superior worship of some of the *Salaf-Al-Saalih*, our righteous predecessors. One book described how one of them complained of growing old and being unable to recite more than the Qur'anic chapters *Al-Baqarah* and *Ali'Imraan* during the night prayer. It also spoke of how the light of faith—that spiritual *noor*—emanated from some of their faces such that when other Muslims saw them, they were immediately reminded of Allah.

SubhaanAllah... I was so deeply moved that tears gathered in my eyes at this description. And in keeping with all my other high hopes of September 2008, I added to my Ramadan schedule the daily supplication to be amongst these people...

"Ruby," my sister said through the receiver just days into Ramadan, "he isn't doing too well."

That was my first hint that I wasn't going to reach all those lofty Ramadan goals I'd set for myself that year. My heart fell, and sadness overwhelmed me as I thought of my younger brother, only twenty-seven years old, now lying in a hospital suffering from cancer.

"They don't think he has much time..."

I grew weak at the news and felt utterly helpless...

But when I hung up, my spirits lifted ever so slightly when I added to my ever-expanding Ramadan list a supplication for my brother's betterment and cure…

"Some*body*, stop me!"

In the quiet of my room, I smiled at the memory. As a teenager, my brother would do a hilarious Jim Carrey impersonation. My siblings and I, no matter how hard we'd try to remain composed, would burst into laughter.

That was my younger brother, spontaneous, and downright funny, *maashaAllah*.

When he was a young boy, sometimes he'd curl up under a blanket just feet from where my sister and I were engaged in deep conversation, and he'd pretend to sleep just to hear what we were saying. If the stories were especially good, he'd drop the pretenses and stand up, letting the blanket fall to the floor, and he'd eagerly ask details about what happened next.

"InshaaAllah," my brother proclaimed what meant *God-willing* from the hospital bed the week I learned of his deteriorating condition, "I'm going to teach Qur'an when I get out of here." He had been studying *Tajweed*, (the rules of reciting Qur'an)via telephone during his sickness, pushing himself to recite the Arabic even when his voice began to give out.

He died just days later…

At the news, I was a bit numb. It didn't seem real.

Innaa lillaahi wa innaa ilayhi raaji'oon. (To Allah we belong, and until Him we all will return)…

I thought of my brother's cackling laughter, his wide smile that seemed to spread over his whole face, and his sneaking in a joke during the most serious moments…

"How are you doing?" I'd asked him one day during the more difficult stages of his illness.

"Well," he'd said, characteristic humor in his tone, "I have my bad days, and my not-so-good days."

We both laughed.

That was one of the last times I spoke to him.

The day of my brother's funeral, we learned that my youngest sister's husband had died suddenly, and we were all caught in a whirlwind of sadness, confusion, and grief…and the second week of Ramadan hadn't even passed.

I tried to read the Qur'an, but my mind kept wandering. I tried to keep up my daily supplications, but my heart felt so empty that it was as if feeling itself had left me. My prayers were mumbled words and mechanical movements, and the tears that wet my cheeks with each motion were not due to *khushoo'*—that deep spiritual concentration and connection with Allah—but due to a gaping melancholy that I couldn't comprehend or overcome.

"When a trial befalls you," an imam had said once during a speech, *"it will be the faith that you already have that will carry you through. There won't be any chance to make up for lost time, and what's in your heart will become exposed..."*

For one of the first times in my life, I understood what he had meant...and I was terrified at what this implied for me. I certainly wasn't feeling a burst of faith lifting my spirits and pushing me through this trial. My fulfillment of all the things I'd zealously put on my Ramadan schedule kept waning each day...

Until finally...I gave up.

The only things I kept up with that Ramadan were things any Muslim should do throughout the year: the five daily prayers, the night prayer, and a few supplications whispered more out of obligation to the Blessed Month than any heartfelt determination on my part. I felt horrible for not even opening the Qur'an for the rest of the month...

> *"[The Angel] Gabriel came to me and said: 'May Allah rub his nose in the dust, that person to whom Ramadan comes and his sins are not forgiven...'"*
> —Prophet Muhammad, peace be upon him (Ibn Majah and Ibn Khuzaimah)

As everyone texted and emailed their congratulations at the announcement of Eid that year, this hadith of the Prophet, peace be upon him, weighed heavily on my heart. I felt like an imposter amongst the sincere believers as I replied with the standard *"wa minna wa minkum"*—the supplication said when anyone said "May Allah accept from you and from us [our worship this Ramadan]."

Accept what? I thought sadly, thinking of my almost non-existent devotion that month. Yes, I had been through a rough time to say the least, but was that any excuse to literally give up on nearly all the goals I'd set for myself? Was that any way to show gratefulness to Allah for at least allowing these tribulations to befall me in the time most suited for patience and tranquility and for turning to Him for help and strength?

O Allah! Put noor *in my heart and on my face, and make me amongst those whom when people see them, they are reminded of You!*

I grunted as I thought of the heartfelt prayer I'd prayed during the first days of Ramadan, naively hoping that the great honor of having spiritual light shining from my face could actually apply to someone as ungrateful and spiritually depraved as me.

That night, I arrived at the *istiraaha*—the villa and plot of land surrounded by a high wall that had been reserved to celebrate Eid that year. (I had dragged myself to the event only on account of my daughter.) As I entered the room full of women, I felt light years away from the joy and spiritual camaraderie that these sisters exuded with their presence alone.

"May Allah accept your worship…" the women said as they greeted each other. I would hear this supplication dozens of times that night, but I drowned it all out. It didn't apply to me.

Minutes after I sat down on the Arab-style floor couch that lined the walls of the villa, I sensed the sister next to me staring, an odd expression on her face. I immediately glanced at her. I was fearful that my Lord had lifted from me the facade I'd worked so hard to maintain, and had revealed to others the spiritual depravation lurking in my heart.

O Allah! Would they actually see the dust on my face?

"What?" I said, smiling in an awkward attempt to mask the trepidation gripping me right then. I already knew my sins. I just didn't want the added humiliation of having them announced to the world…

"MaashaAllah," she said, "you have so much *noor* on your face."

But…

"Yes, *maashaAllah*," another sister said, her eyes glistening in admiration as she smiled up at me from where she sat on the carpeted floor.

"So beautiful," someone else said, smiling and shaking her head in deep reflection. "*MaashaAllah*. So much *noor*."

> *By the glorious morning light,*
> *And by the night when it is still,*
> *Your Guardian Lord has not forsaken you,*
> *Nor is He displeased…*

I cried when, after that night, I read these Qur'anic verses from *Soorah Al-Duhaa*. My experience that Eid highlighted for me a new meaning to the vastness of Allah's mercy and forgiveness that He promises believers during the month of Ramadan.

I had given up on myself during the Month of Mercy. Yet my Lord—the Most Gracious, the Most Merciful, the All-Forgiving— had not given up on me…

So, dear brother and sister, whoever you are and wherever you may be, and no matter how incredibly far you fear you may have fallen short in your spiritual journey, know that your Creator's mercy and forgiveness reach far beyond where even you yourself made effort to reach.

And even though you may be a bit disappointed in your faults and shortcomings, this is my prayer and hope for you…

May Allah accept from you your worship, however little or much it may be, and may He put on your face *noor*—that spiritual light of faith— so that when people see you, they are reminded of Him.

Original version published via saudilife.net

2
'But I Don't Want Forgiveness'

◆

Some years ago, I was sitting with a friend of mine and she started telling me about her struggles with hijab after becoming Muslim. She had grown up Christian and accepted Islam while she was in college.

"For me, hijab was the hardest thing," she said. "I just didn't want to wear it. So I made every excuse I could. 'It's too hot.' 'I can't breathe'." She shook her head, remembering. "But the funny thing is, I didn't realize I didn't want to cover.

"Until one day I was talking to some sisters and I was making the same excuses. And the sisters started trying to convince me, but for everything they said, I had an answer. And we kept going back and forth. But then a sister said something that I really couldn't respond to." She paused. "'Just make *du'aa*. Pray that Allah makes it easy for you'."

Her eyes grew distant, reflecting. "When she said that, I didn't know what to say. In the back of my mind, I knew that if I asked Allah for help, I would wear hijab. And that's when I knew I didn't really want to cover. I didn't even ask Allah to help me. Because I didn't want Him to."

When I hear stories like these, I think of the depths of the human heart. I think of how we think we know ourselves and our intentions. But, really, we don't.

For almost every one of us, there's something we know we need to change but simply won't. The issue may involve not wearing hijab, not praying regularly, watching inappropriate TV and movies, intermingling, having "boyfriends" or "girlfriends"... And for each, we have a convenient excuse, if we bother to make excuses at all.

But in Ramadan, a lot of unpleasant things come to surface because the devils are chained and the depths of our hearts are exposed.

Yet most of us still manage to wriggle out of obedience to Allah, and the excuses abound...

There's no point in wearing hijab in Ramadan if I know I'm just going to take it off later...
I don't want to be a hypocrite...
I know myself, and I'm not ready to change my life...

But in each excuse, there's one key component that's missing.
Allah.
I don't mean His name is absent. For most of us, it's actually Allah's name we use to justify our wrong.
Allah is Forgiving. Allah knows my heart. Allah's my judge...
Or our favorite...
When I change, I'll do it for Allah, not because people asked me to...
Yet Allah says, *"And make not Allah's (name) an excuse in your oaths against doing good, or acting rightly..."* (2:224).

When we're not blaming Allah for our sins, we're blaming our natural human weakness. And it's true; humans are weak. But the truth is that this isn't our chief shortcoming.

But human weakness *is* the chief shortcoming for those with high *emaan*.

Those with low *emaan* have as their chief shortcoming a diseased heart.

The strong believers constantly strive to do what's right, but because of human weakness, they inevitably fall short. But their energy is spent striving against sin, not giving in to it.

The weakest believers don't even bother striving; they're quite comfortable in their life of sin. Their energy is spent defending their sin, not fighting against it.

...I don't want forgiveness. I don't want to change. I like the wrong I'm doing...

This is what it really boils down to. Otherwise, we'd just make *du'aa*, and pray that Allah makes it easy for us to do what's right, even if we fall short at times.

But it starts with wanting change. And that's not an easy thing for the human heart, especially for those of us content with our low *emaan* and life of sin.

Yet...

All will be forgiven during the month of Ramadan, except those who do not want to be forgiven.
And who does not want to be forgiven?
Those who do not ask.

The month of Ramadan is, more than anything, a month of opportunity. It is a time to set right things that are wrong. It's a time to change course, even as you've no idea how you'll walk that new path. It's a time to ask for change, to beg for change, to *cry* for it—even if part of you doesn't even want it.

And it's okay if you have no idea how you'll manage wearing hijab, praying regularly, shutting off that TV, or leaving alone those "cute" girls or guys.

It's okay, because it's not you you're turning to for help.

It's Allah.

And Allah is able to do all things.

Let us remember, too, that Allah is All-Forgiving. But, of course, to benefit from Allah's Forgiveness, we first have to want it. And wanting forgiveness isn't just saying we want it, or just uttering a prayer. It means we regret our sin. It means we hate our sin. And it means we take every step to avoid it.

And we never give up fighting against it.

That's what it means to want Allah's forgiveness.

That's what it means to ask for it.

So it is upon each of us to closely examine our lives—and hearts—and ask ourselves a simple question.

Do you want forgiveness?

If our answer is yes, we know Who to turn to for help and guidance.

If our answer is no… well, there's nothing for us to do except what we've always been doing.

Previously published via saudilife.net

3

Got a Survival Kit? Help for Muslim Apostates

◆

"I'm just calling to let you know I'm not Muslim anymore," the woman said to me after I picked up the phone, "and I'm cutting off contact with all Muslims except you."

This was one of the most difficult conversations I've ever had.

My heart ached for this woman; I knew her story all too well.

I had been in the "frontline" with her as she tried to find her place in the Muslim community, and repeatedly failed. masjid after masjid, community after community, yet so few were willing to assist her in securing a roof over her head and food each night; and she had been just eighteen years old at the time she was repeatedly turned away.

She had accepted Islam in a small Northern town when she was still in high school, got kicked out of school because she wore hijab, and moved to the D.C. metropolitan area with nothing but her name, her faith in Allāh, and her knowledge that a "strong Muslim community" was there to receive her…

"We don't discriminate against *any*one," the masjid administrator said with pride. Other board members chimed in from time to time. "Sister so-and-so teaches kindergarten, Sister so-and-so works in the daycare, and Brother so-and-so…"

I sat speechless as I listened to them list the commitment of about five "comfortable, happy, dedicated" Americans who worked at their Muslim school or who were regular participants in the community. I felt like I was listening to a Southern self-proclaimed anti-racist in the 1950s tell me their "black folk were happy", proof being that Black folk smiled at them each day and always "without protest" used the separate Jim Crow facilities.

What made the board's proclamations so heartbreaking was that they actually believed themselves.

I tried another approach: I mentioned how even non-Muslim communities and schools set up multicultural awareness programs and offered cultural sensitivity training and—

"That's from *jahiliyyah* (ignorant of the guidance from God)," a board member said before I could finish speaking.

What?

Though I was deeply offended, I gathered my composure enough to remind myself why I was there.

It was then that I realized I could use this moment to make them understand my point. After all, even word choice created cultural barriers. And since I knew how much brotherhood and sisterhood meant to them, I expressed how their words made me feel as if they were putting up a wall between us.

"And *your* words make me feel as if *you* are putting up a wall..."

Little did the board know, I had not called this meeting on my own account; days before, several community members (a multiracial group of mostly converts to Islam) felt I could meet with the board as a "last resort" to help the community. They'd imagined that my good standing in the community would allow the board to hear the concerns with open hearts and ears...

"If you ever have any more concerns," a board member said as she followed me to the door (The meeting ended once it was clear we were getting nowhere), "feel free to come talk to us at any time." She wore a broad smile that exuded warmth and kindness. "We're always open to suggestions." She placed a hand on my shoulder. "And please know we love you like a sister..."

I tried not to break into sobs right then...

"*Were you at Jumu'ah last Friday?*" a masjid board member said to another. "*Ohhh, it was so beautiful. A young American girl took her shahaadah. We were all in tears...*"

It was only by the mercy of Allāh that after the apostate woman and I talked for some time, she decided to come back to Islam. But she remained discontented and distant from the Muslim community after that.

However, her story is actually a rare one. Apostates generally don't give Muslims phone calls to say "I'm through." But nearly all apostates give Muslims warning calls before they leave...

The first warning call is quite unambiguous: They ask for help—literally.

How can I learn to pray?
What activities are there in the community?
What do I need to know as a new Muslim?
Do I have to cover?
What do I tell my parents?

Is it true that Islam teaches such-and-such?

Given the popularity of *da'wah* (inviting to Islam) programs in masjids across America, it's quite shocking that so few have after-the-*da'wah* programs. Unfortunately, convincing a non-Muslim to accept Islam is the "end of the journey" in most Masjids...while this moment is just the beginning for the one who accepts Islam.

Too many Masjids are content with providing teary-eyed after-*Jumu'ah* entertainment for the soft-hearted congregation more than they are concerned with providing a helping hand to the one evoking tears in Muslims' eyes. I suppose we can't get enough of hearing that heartfelt "I bear witness..." echoed through the microphone...

But where do all these new *shahaadah*s (Muslims converts) go after that tearful *Jumu'ah*?

One of them gave me a call once to let me know.

My suggestion to any Muslim who wants to help stop the revolving door of "Muslim today, apostate tomorrow" is to get a survival kit—one for yourself and one for the struggling Muslim you meet.

Here's what *your* survival kit should contain:

1. A three-sentence instruction guide that essentially reads: "Forget getting the support of the masjid or 'model Muslim community' you're so fond up, and just roll up your sleeves. You're on your own in this one, I'm afraid. If you have plenty of spare time and are not prone to bouts of laryngitis, then set up a weekly or monthly meeting to share with them your concerns and suggestions."
2. A merciful, patient, determined heart. This is going to be your lifeline during this project. *How so?* ...Well, start the project, and *bi'idhnillaah* (God willing), you'll see.
3. Thick skin. Ever heard the saying "You asked for it"? Well, if you ask new or struggling Muslims their needs and concerns, be prepared to actually hear what they have to say. These Muslims have a lot on their minds and hearts, and it's not always pretty. The good news is that if they're talking to you, then most likely they actually *want* to keep their *emaan* (faith).
4. A prayer mat and several supplications from the Qur'an and Sunnah. (Prayer and *du'a* for your own soul and steadfastness upon Islam will be indispensable every step of the way.)
5. Some really balanced, knowledgeable Muslim friends. (You'll be needing lots of advice and support yourself.)

Here's what *their* survival kit should contain:

1. A one-sentence instruction sheet that essentially reads: "Forget getting the support of other Muslims, and just focus on getting the guidance and support of Allāh."
2. A "back to the basics" approach to holding on to your Islam. This means you focus on primarily three things during your "recovery period": studying *Tawheed* (the Oneness of Allāh), establishing regular prayer (with sincerity and concentration), and reading Qur'an (in your native language and, if possible, in Arabic too).
3. A prayer mat and a few supplications from the Qur'an and Sunnah. (Prayer and *du'a* for guidance and steadfastness upon Islam will be indispensable during this time—and at every stage of life.)
4. Willingness to, if you have doubts or questions, ask... not just any Muslim, but one you feel you can trust. (Unfortunately, not all Muslims are understanding or honest).
5. The realization that this internal "fight for spiritual survival" is a lifelong process that will never end until you meet Allah. (But the good news is this: It does get easier if you persevere.)

If we keep these "survival kits" on hand and actually use them, perhaps we can help someone on the verge of leaving Islam. Then maybe one day we'll pick up our phone and hear: "I'm just calling to let you know I'm still Muslim. Thank you for helping me realize I made the right choice."
And when we get all teary-eyed at hearing this heartfelt testimony, we'll know we didn't abandon the one who evoked the tears.

Previously published via muslimmatters.org

4
'But I Don't Trust God'

◆

"But I don't trust God," the man said.

He was a neighbor of ours and had just learned that his wife was terminally ill. Though the man was Christian, my husband had advised him to turn to God in prayer and to place his trust in Him...

"You cannot even begin to understand the depths of confusion caused by believing that God is a man," my father had once said while reflecting on his former life as a Christian.

It was these words that came to mind when I watched a 1997 interview with the famous actor Bill Cosby after his son was killed, and he said, "God can't control everything." And even the interviewer couldn't conceal being taken aback by his words...

"You don't trust God?" my husband asked our neighbor.

The man averted his gaze. "No," he said, unveiling frustration right then. "No, I don't."

Many Muslims may find such sacrilegious statements incomprehensible. It's difficult to imagine how a person can live a life ostensibly believing in God yet neither trusting Him nor believing He controls all affairs.

That's because they don't believe in God in the right way, we may conclude.

And that's true. When people do not know their Creator in the proper sense, this ignorance disrupts their relationship with God.

Allah says,

"They [the Jews and Christians] took their rabbis and monks to be their lords besides Allah and [they also took as their Lord] Christ, the son of Mary. Yet they were commanded to worship one God... "
(*Al-Tawbah*, 9:31)

Naturally, the religious teachings of humans influence far more than what is deemed lawful and prohibited or the manner one worships God. These flawed teachings further influence the role God plays in followers' lives...and whether or not they trust Him or believe He controls all affairs.

"Make *du'aa* for me this Ramadan," the woman said to me.

"Of course," I said. "And make *du'aa* for me too."

A shy smile toyed at her lips. "No," she said quietly. "You're a better Muslim than me. I think Allah will answer your prayers. I'm not a good Muslim."

I'm often at a loss for words when Muslims speak like this. If having our prayers answered depended entirely on "being a good Muslim," then certainly I myself wouldn't be inclined to raise my hands in supplication.

"Put your trust in Allah, *ukhti*. He hears and answers prayers."

She averted her gaze. "Yeah, okay…"

But her hesitance conveyed sentiments similar to those our neighbor expressed…

So where did our lessons about God go wrong? Why do we have the Qur'an and Sunnah yet still hold on to a flawed view of the Creator? Where did we learn that struggling with human faults and sins makes us unworthy of Allah's love and forgiveness?

Allah says,

"Say, O My slaves who have wronged their souls! Despair not of the mercy of Allah. Verily, Allah forgives all sins. Truly, He is Oft-Forgiving, Most Merciful." (Al-Zumar, 39:53)

He also tells us,

"O son of Adam, so long as you call upon Me and ask of Me, I shall forgive you for what you have done, and I shall not mind. O son of Adam, were your sins to reach the clouds of the sky and were you then to ask forgiveness of Me, I would forgive you. O son of Adam, were you to come to Me with sins nearly as great as the earth and were you then to face Me, ascribing no partner to Me, I would bring you forgiveness nearly as great as it."

—Qudsi hadith (Al-Tirmidhi and Ahmad, authenticated by Al-Albani)

Yes, it is true that our sins put us at risk of not having our prayers answered. But it is also true that no human is without sin.

The Prophet, *sallallaahu'alayhi wa sallam*, said, "All of the children of Adam sin, and the best of those who sin are those who constantly repent" (Bukhari).

When Muslims fall into despair and depression due to their sins, they aren't too different from those who don't trust God or who believe that God can't control everything.

After all, if we trust Allah, we know He hears and answers our prayers, and if we believe Allah is All-Powerful, then we know He has control over all affairs…

And we know it is not beyond Allah's capacity to forgive us, no matter how numerous or major our sins.

Often it is the words of people or the whispers of Shaytaan that cripple us in our weakest moments. Thus, we imagine that even a month as blessed as Ramadan and a Mercy as vast as that bestowed from Al-Raheem—the Most Merciful—is beyond our reach.

At these moments, we become dangerously similar to the followers of innovated religions who trust the views of mortal beings over that of the Creator…

And sometimes that mortal view is our own.

We may think of how weak and "bad" we are in comparison to "good Muslims," or we may believe the harsh words of someone who made us feel like a "bad Muslim," and we somehow imagine these views reflect our fate more than that of Allah's promise of mercy and forgiveness.

And this imagination may even block our inspiration to participate fully in the month of Ramadan….because we think its blessings and promises of Paradise are for "somebody else."

Yet the Prophet, *sallallaahu'alayhi wa sallam*, said: "In every day and every night, during the month of Ramadan, there are people to whom Allah grants freedom from the Fire, and there is for every Muslim a supplication which he can make and will be granted" (al-Bazzaar, Ahmad and Ibn Majah; *saheeh*).

So rest assured, O child of Adam, that *inshaaAllah* one of those Muslims is you.

How do I know?

Well…I'm Muslim.

So I trust Allah.

Original version published via saudilife.net

5

Reality of Ramadan: You Might Not Benefit

◆

I returned to my dormitory room after a full day of classes—and fasting. I was exhausted. Outside was dark, and my stomach grumbled. I had eaten only a little at *iftaar* because I had been so busy with schoolwork and meetings.

As I settled at my desk with a bagel and some grapes, I glanced at the clock. It was almost time for *Ishaa*. Already, I felt dread knotting in my chest. I could barely keep up with praying my five prayers on time; how would I pray *Tarawih*…alone?

I drew in a deep breath and exhaled, in that moment mentally scolding myself for my doubts. *I will pray Tarawih every night this Ramadan*, I told myself, *no matter what.*

An hour later I was facing the *Qiblah* as I completed my first two units of *Tarawih*. Heaviness weighed on my limbs and my mind wandered. *How many more to go?* I asked myself in irritation.

I mentally blocked out the question and moved on to the next set of prayers…and the next…and the next.

When I finished I almost collapsed in relief.

I was *finally* done. I met the warmth of my bed feeling as if a weight had been lifted from my shoulders…

And an even weightier load put in its place.

That was the last time I prayed *Tarawih* that Ramadan.

"Whoever observed prayer at night during Ramadan because of faith and seeking his reward from Allah, his previous sins will be forgiven" (Muslim).

It took a series of repeated spiritual failures like the one I experienced as a first-year American college student before I finally faced the painful reality I had been avoiding for so long: Ramadan just wasn't what it used to be.

My parents had become Muslim the year I was born, so all the years preceding my living alone for the first time were filled with Islam in the house.

As a child I fasted the long summer days along with my older siblings and my parents. I enjoyed the burst of pride I felt upon waking early in the morning and breaking fast at the end of the day. I felt like such a "grownup" savoring the sweetness of dates and cold water, and praying shoulder-to-shoulder next to my big sisters. I also felt a sense of purpose sitting down and reading a thirtieth of the English Qur'an and reflecting on its verses. And I was unable to contain my sense of accomplishment upon finishing the entire book at the end of the month.

Although as a child fasting was not always easy (especially during the summer when the sun set close to nine o'clock at night), I recall Ramadan being such a tranquil month, and I was often in awe at the spirituality I felt emanating from within.

As I worshipped Allah, at moments I really felt a sense of camaraderie with the rest of the world—the sun rising each morning, the stillness of the grass outside, and the smiling faces of believers...

To me, Ramadan had always been...

Miraculous...

Until it wasn't anymore.

One day the Messenger of Allah, *sallallaahu'alayhi wa sallam*, ascended the mimbar and said: "Ameen. Ameen. Ameen." The Companions asked, "O Messenger of Allah, why did you do that?" He said, "[The Angel] Jibreel said to me, 'May Allah rub his nose in the dust—the person to whom Ramadan comes and his sins are not forgiven,' and I said, 'Ameen'..." (Ibn Khuzaymah -1888; Tirmidhi-3545; Ahmad -7444).

When I first heard this hadith, I shuddered.

Was it that my loss of tranquility in Ramadan was due to my being amongst those about whom the angel spoke in this hadith?

...I didn't want to think about it.

It has been more than fifteen years since I spent my first Ramadan away from home. And although I've been blessed with many a tranquil Ramadan thereafter—filled with nights standing in *Tarawih* and crying to Allah—I don't think I've ever recovered from the spiritual loss I suffered that year.

Even now as Ramadan has arrived and I have a family of my own, I feel my chest constrict and tears of apprehension fill my eyes...

"When the month of Ramadan starts, the gates of Paradise are opened and the gates of Hell are closed, and the devils are chained" (Bukhari).

Will I suffer like I did before?

Will I turn from the gates of Paradise, shutting my eyes to my faults and sins?

Will I stand eagerly—and patiently—at the gates of Hell...

Awaiting the Blessed Month to end?

...I shiver at that thought.

"O Allah! Protect me from myself!" I pray.

Ramadan is the most feared and eagerly awaited month of the year, I wrote in my diary a few years ago.

And for me, it is.

...Because now I know all too well that there is nothing "miraculous" about the Month of Mercy.

There is no tranquility that will fall into your lap. There is no spirituality that will settle over you while you sit idle...

Only those who want Ramadan's blessings will receive them. Only those who want Allah's forgiveness will be granted it.

And only those who want Paradise will enter it.

And for me, that is the most terrifying—and welcomed—reality of all...

That it is possible for any human—whose death is the only imminent certainty of life—to actually live a single day on this earth, or an entire month of Ramadan, without benefiting from it...

And that it is possible for any human—who sincerely turns to Allah before that moment of certainty—to be granted forgiveness greater than his faith and deeds deserve.

And Allah offers us both in this Blessed Month.

Which will you choose?

Previously published via saudilife.net

6
Strawberry Prayers: A Lesson of Ramadan Love

♦

My little brother loved strawberries. Whenever my father would come home with a cardboard box full of fruit, the sweet scent would seep through the slots on the side, and my little brother would come running. His chubby legs moved him swiftly up the stairs and landed him first to the dining room table, where my father would be setting down the box.
"Daddy, can I have some strawberries?" my little brother would ask eagerly, eyeing the box with widening eyes as my father removed the lid. My father would smile and rub my brother's head, saying, "After we pray."

Though only five years old, my brother would hurry to prepare for prayer and wait impatiently for the rest of the family to come to the living room to join him.

But prayer was not so urgent when there were no strawberries in the house...

That Ramadan, my parents decided to encourage my little brother to pray *Tarawih*—the night prayer—with the family, but he always had an excuse...or he was just too tired. Then one evening my father said to him, "If you pray with us, you can have strawberries when we finish."

That did it. My little brother stood in line alongside his older brothers, and we heard not a single peep from him until we turned our heads to the left, signaling the end of prayer. But before we could even complete the movement, my little brother was already asking our father, "Daddy, can I have strawberries now?"

Each night of Ramadan passed like this until my little brother said early one night before the time for *Tarawih* came, "Daddy, will we be praying the strawberry prayers tonight?"

His reference to *Tarawih* as the "strawberry prayers" drew light chuckles out of my mother and father and suppressed giggles from me and my siblings.

As we entered the last days of Ramadan, my little brother was often the first one ready for *Tarawih*, and he'd always eagerly ask, "Are we going to pray the strawberry prayers tonight?"

Though it was the cutest thing to see the eagerness on his face to get those strawberries after prayer, I was often left wondering what would happen when there were no strawberries to offer…

Then one night there were no strawberries in the house, and my brother knew this. I worried that he wouldn't pray with us though of course our parents wouldn't compel him to. But shortly after the family prayed 'Ishaa, the last of the five obligatory prayers, my brother entered the living room. To our surprise, he asked with all sincerity and eagerness, "Daddy, are we going to pray the strawberry prayers tonight?"

My father's expression was one of pleasant surprise as he realized that my brother had come to love the *Tarawih* prayer, with or without strawberries. My father smiled and said, "Yes, we will."

After we finished prayer, I stole a look at my little brother, and there was a look of satisfaction on his face. This warmed my heart…

The sweetness of prayer had become more pleasing to him than the sweetness of strawberries.

The Sweetness of Prayer

It has been more than twenty years since my little brother began praying *Tarawih* on his own, but till today I think of that Ramadan; and I can't help smiling as I think of the "strawberry prayers." But what stays with me is far deeper than the warmth I had in my heart for the memories.

Today, I am grateful that Allah allowed me to witness the love of prayer blossom in a child's heart. And as a parent, I understand the deep lesson my parents were passing on to my brother—and to all of us.

In order to instill in children's hearts the love of what Allah loves, we ourselves must love what Allah loves…and we should communicate this love with something "sweet" that children will always associate with beloved acts like prayer and fasting.

No, this love need not be communicated with strawberries after every prayer or with any tangible "sweet". But it must be communicated, even if only through a smile and a rub of the head when it's time for prayer…allowing children to see us happy and content when we're about to worship Allah.

As for me, till today, when I line up for *Tarawih* prayer, I can still hear my brother saying, "Daddy, are we going to pray the strawberry prayers tonight?" And I see my father smile, rub my brother's head, and say, "Yes, we will."

And when I raise my hands to start prayer, I remember the sweet taste of strawberries and think, *I can't wait to taste the sweetest fruit of all…*

Jannah, the eternal Paradise that Allah prepared for those who, on earth, tasted the sweetness of faith.

With this inspiration, I hope to eagerly pray the night prayers as long as I'm alive—in Ramadan and beyond. And when my soul is taken upon Islam, God-willing, then perhaps I myself, like my brother, will eagerly ask, "Can I have the fruits of Jannah now?"

Previously published via onislam.net

7
Walking Wounded
Umm Zakiyyah & Na'ima B. Robert Discuss Spiritual Crisis

◆

"For some, this period [of religious development] was characterized by increased insularity, intolerance, and estrangement, sometimes from family...At the time, this felt right...But a curious thing happened to many of us as we aged...We began to see ourselves as individuals rather than members of homogenous 'whole'. And, of course, this led to friction as others saw us change, evolve and grow in ways they had not expected. Or, in more painful examples, the trauma had a negative impact on our practice of Islam which, in turn, led to even greater friction and estrangement from those we had once felt so close to. These are the sisters I term the 'walking wounded'."
—Na'ima B. Robert, "Editor's Space," SISTERS Magazine (March 2013)

UZ: What went wrong? That's the question I ask when I look around me and see so many wounded brothers and sisters struggling to hold on to their Islam, some who've simply let go. It's a question I even ask myself when I'm deeply pained by my own experiences with Muslims and our never-ending quest to champion 'pure Islam' in the world.

Na'ima, when I read your editor's note in the March issue of SISTERS, it brought tears to my eyes; *maashaAllah*, may Allah bless you for writing it. I think so many of us, whether we were born into Muslim homes or accepted Islam later in life, can understand the profound implications of 'walking wounded'—sometimes on a very personal level, within our own lives or the lives of those we love.

Can you explain this term 'walking wounded' and what inspired you to use this vivid analogy?

NB: *JazakAllahu khairan* for your kind words about the editorial. I was inspired to write it after learning of some severe trials that some sisters I knew were facing. Now, the thing with trials is this: if you encounter them when your *iman* is relatively strong, they can actually serve to make it stronger. Greater reliance on Allah SWT, increased supplication, a reminder of the true nature of this world; these are some of the positive side-effects of experiencing trials when your *iman* is in fairly good shape. On the flip side, if your *iman* is already weakened, these trials may wear it down even further, leading us to question our beliefs and doubt in Allah's wisdom. Often, in these cases, there are feelings of disappointment or anger and these are directed at the Muslims who have either not helped the person who is suffering, or made the situation worse in some way. This translates into a generalised feeling of disillusionment and distrust of Muslims.

UZ: How common is this 'walking wounded' experience for Muslims today?

NB: I think there are a lot of Muslims hurting, a lot of Muslims suffering in their own quiet ways. And I am not referring here to suffering brought on by political upheaval. I'm talking about ordinary Muslims, in everyday life, suffering. And for me, what makes their pain all the more poignant and unsettling, is that, as far as we were concerned, it was *never meant to be this way*. You mentioned 'pure Islam' earlier and I read that with a wry smile. We thought that, once we accepted Islam, and did our very best to practice it according to the Sunnah etc, life would be better. Not perfect, because a perfect, happy life is reserved for *Jannah* - may we all meet there, *ameen*. But sisters were prepared to sacrifice, to 'downsize', especially within marriages. We were prepared to give up work, to obey, to concentrate on the home, on childrearing and, for quite a few, accept polygamy and all that that entails. But, in return, I think we hoped for a good, honest life, a life of dignity, yes, we expected that, as sisters. And, from what I see today, it is the gap between those hopes and expectations and the reality that many sisters have had to face, that has led to the 'walking wounded' phenomenon. I think a lot of married sisters are hurting, I think a lot of divorced sisters are hurting, but there is no way for them to address these feelings in our communities. There is no way for them to demand justice from within the community. And this is not confined to sisters. Brothers have faced it, too, with other brothers who they came to rely on or with their families. I am thinking in particular of brothers who have not been allowed access to their children after divorce. A recent Facebook post brought this matter to my attention and, *subhanAllah*, so often we think that the brothers can't be hurt, that they have the upper hand in all situations. This discussion on custody opened my eyes to the fact that this is not always the case and that sisters can also be vindictive and manipulative, when it suits them.

UZ: What do you believe is leading to such a dramatic shift from a spiritual high to spiritual trauma? Is there something we as individuals or communities are doing wrong? Was there something wrong in how or what we learned about Islam in our formative years of seeking knowledge?

NB: There are a few things to consider here: firstly, I think our expectations were perhaps too high. But then again, if you can't expect a lot from the Muslims, 'the best nation', who can you expect it from? But maybe what we wanted 'the community' to deliver, especially in communities with a high convert/returnee population, was unrealistic. I think that, in an ordinary Islamic context, much of the support that we feel we need from the masjid is supposed to come from the family. And if that support isn't there, we feel the failings of the masjid all the more keenly. I also think that, in some communities, there is too much emphasis on outward conformity to Islamic rules, and not enough on building a sincere and rich relationship with Allah SWT and cleansing ourselves, looking inward. The two sides are needed for a balanced Islamic identity. For many, it is easier to cloak oneself in the garb of piety than to strive to truly embody it. The only trouble with that is, when your conviction is tested for one reason or another, you often don't have the spiritual fortitude to withstand the trial, and Allah knows best.

UZ: When I talk to some sisters who are on the verge of leaving Islam, I notice that for the vast majority of them, they are so deeply hurt by what they've experienced that there is strong aversion to being around Muslims or hearing Islamic lectures or talks. Have you noticed anything similar? What is your perspective on why this happens?

NB: I have definitely noticed this and, again, I put it down to the disillusionment and disappointment felt by such sisters. It's like, 'Yeah, I heard all that talk before but I know the reality now.' For instance, if you feel that the Muslims have failed you as a woman, the last thing you want to hear is someone talking about how Islam honours women. If you have been denied your rights, the last thing you want to hear is a lecture on women's rights in Islam. I feel that there comes a time for realness. And that realness is acknowledging the gap between the ideals that Islam holds and the *reality* that Muslims face. By all means, call to Islamic ideals, teach them, remind the Muslims about them. But you can't stop there. If you do not deal with the reality on the ground, the *truth* that people are living and tasting every day, you are doing the community a disservice and mocking the idea of 'living Islam'. Because it's much harder to deal with those truths, much harder to come to terms with those uncomfortable realities. But we must or those wounds will continue to fester and start to infect other parts of the community. This is me talking about translating Islamic ideals into practical solutions that will impact people's lived realities.

UZ: So often when there are spiritual crises amongst Muslims, a lot of blame is placed on masjids and communities as a whole. But on an individual level, how can brothers and sisters help stop or lessen spiritual trauma amongst fellow Muslims?

NB: As far as I am concerned, it is upon those of us who have been blessed with the ability to practise Islam to develop empathy. We are so cold, so unfeeling, so aloof. This allows us to distance ourselves from the wounded ones, to point fingers and sit in judgement. It is one thing to see or hear of someone's sin and, privately, seek refuge in Allah SWT from falling into it, or thank Allah SWT that He has not tested us with that. We make a private judgement about that action: do we hold it to be *halal* or *haram* for ourselves? Every Muslim must do this so that we can remain unequivocal about Allah's laws. However, when it comes to the person who has committed that sin, our judgement should become empathy, seeking to understand, to support, to help them through it, guiding and advising them through word *and* deed. We give *'naseehah'* – reminders, *ayat* of Qur'an or *ahadith* – because it's easier. To me, I have come to see this as shorthand for 'It's easier for me to remind you of a hadith than get involved in the mess of your life or actually be there for you in any meaningful, practical way.' That may sound harsh but, often, this is the way it comes across to the person being 'advised' in this way.

UZ: I agree. I too have noticed this. I think those who are blessed with the ability to practice Islam but do not have empathy for others are neither practicing Islam nor understanding it. So perhaps, the vast majority of us are in one way or another 'walking wounded'—some of us through imagining that we're practicing Islam when we're not, and others through consciously giving up on "doing right" due to spiritual exhaustion and confusion.

And Allah knows best.

May Allah purify our hearts and return us to true faith such that our belief in Him heals any wounds we may experience on this difficult journey toward meeting Him.

Originally published via muslimmatters.org

PART II
Hope for the Confused and Sinful

You don't need to have all the answers.
You just need to trust the One who does.
　　　　　　—from the journal of Umm Zakiyyah

8
Aim High By Aiming Low
Setting Realistic Minimums Instead of Lofty Goals

◆

It's something I learned the hard way. I wasn't going to meet all those lofty goals I'd set for myself after all. In youthful (or prideful) innocence and under the fire of a motivated and determined heart, I set many "sky high," reach-for-the-stars goals, telling myself all the things *I* would do differently than everyone else to actually *get* what I wanted from life—personally in my marriage and family, socially with my friends and acquaintances, financially with my business pursuits, and yes, even spiritually with my practice of Islam. *I* was going to be different from everyone else…

Until I found that I wasn't.

I was already a wife and mother when I penned to myself this painful, intentionally sarcastic journal entry: "And so, you are human after all."

But here's the interesting part: Once I embraced the reality that I was no different or better than anyone else, even those I could only pray I would never be, I settled for some realistic "minimums" instead reaching for those stars.

Thus, my entire outlook on life shifted: Instead of striving to be the lifesaver overlooking life's beach, so to speak, I was striving to just keep my head above the water so I wouldn't drown (or pull anyone else down with me).

Ironically, as I settled for who I really was (a mere human riddled with numerous faults who was utterly incapable of escaping *any* of life's disappointments–even the dark spiritual degeneration of the human heart), something miraculous happened: Those once "lofty" goals I'd given up on actually came into view…

And I actually reached many of them without even trying to.

Honestly, when this happened, I was a bit shaken up. I was terrified to be honest. Though, I can't explain this feeling except to say, as many have before me: *It is not the depths of our weaknesses that terrify us most, but the depths of our strengths.*

It is a scary thought to know just how powerful you are as a human, to know that yes, you *can* be amongst the best wives or husbands, the best mothers or fathers, the best businesswomen or men, and yes even amongst the best Muslims...

Because once you get a glimpse into that nearly limitless human potential you have within, there's no way to escape personal and spiritual success—except by sinking into self denial.

Traversing this period of my life taught me a lot about the human soul: When we're not doing what we're supposed to do or when we're not doing the absolute *best* we can—personally and spiritually— it's not because we're weak or incapable or not "gifted" or spiritually "strong" like others. It's because we've made a conscious, deliberate decision *not* to.

This realization hit me so profoundly that I was once on the verge of tears when I said to a companion of mine, "I've come to realize that any human who enters the Fire in the Hereafter enters it only after having seen Paradise in front of them. But then they decide quite frankly, 'No, I want Hell Fire instead.'" A bit overcome with emotion herself, my friend grew pensively quiet and said, "That is so true... That is so true..."

Imagine all the times so many of us have talked about wanting so badly to wake up late at night and pray *Tahajjud*, the voluntary night prayer, if only we could just wake up! And then one night, as if miraculously, Allah wakes us up until we're fully awake and we glance at the clock; and the glowing numbers are a conspicuous reminder—and gift—from Allah telling us, "Now's your chance."

And then our heart falls in dread (because we want more sleep!) and we pull the covers over our heads. And even as we're not as tired as we'd like to be, we shut our eyes (literally and spiritually) trying to drift off and forget we ever had that chance...

Once, the Prophet, sallallaahu'alayhi wa sallam, *was seen crying. When the Companions saw his sadness, they asked, "What makes you cry, O Messenger of Allah?"*

The Prophet said, "I miss my brothers."

They said, "Aren't we your brothers, O Messenger of Allah?"

He said, "No, you are my Companions. My brothers are those who will come after me and they will believe in me without seeing me" (Tabarani and Al-Hakim*).*

The Messenger of Allah, sallallaahu'alayhi wa sallam, *also said,*

"Some people will come on the Day of Judgment and their emaan *[faith] will be outstanding. Its light will shine from their chests and from*

their right hands. So it will be said to them, 'Glad tidings for you today. Assalaamu'alaykum [peace be upon you] and goodness for you. Enter into it [Paradise] forever!' So the angels and the Prophets will be jealous of the love of Allah for them."

So the Companions asked, "Who are they, O Messenger of Allah?"

He replied, "They are not from us and they are not from you. You are my companions but they are my beloved. They will come after you and will find the Book made redundant by the people, and a Sunnah which has been killed by them. So they will grab hold of the Book and the Sunnah and revive them [both].

"So they will read and teach them [the Qur'an and Sunnah] to the people and they will experience in that path a punishment more severe and more ugly than what you [O my Companions] have experienced. Indeed, the emaan of one of them is equivalent to the emaan of forty of you...

Because you found a helper towards the truth [the Prophet living amongst you] and they will find no helper towards the truth...

Then the Prophet said, "O Allah give them the Victory and make them my close friends in Jannah [Paradise]" (Reported by Ahmed #17561, chain #77; hasan according to Ibn Hajr).

When I first heard this hadith, I cried. I couldn't imagine being amongst the brethren of the Prophet or amongst those who held *emaan* forty times as much as some of the Companions.

Yet, as I experienced the depths of vulnerability in my life and faith, Allah gave me a small glimpse into the depths of my strength as a person and a believer.

So today, I have hope.

And my renewed hope rests in the promise of Allah that He's given to the believers again and again throughout the Qur'an:

"And give glad tidings to those who believe and do righteous deeds, that for them will be Gardens under which rivers flow..."
—*Al-Baqarah (2:25)*

As I struggle as a believer in this world, I certainly falter more than I like (or should), but continue to hope for Paradise. And I hold on to this hope by sticking to these five spiritual guidelines to keep me on the right path, *bi'idhnillaah*:

1. Build your day and life around *Salaah*—the five daily prayers—and gather your strength and guidance from them.
2. At least once daily, ask for forgiveness and make *du'aa* [prayerful supplication] regarding your worldly life and your

Hereafter.
3. Find time, some way somehow, to get up and pray at night on a regular basis, even if only once a week, and even if only for three units of *Witr*, and even if sitting down while you're unwell.
4. Read a certain amount of Qur'an every single day.
5. Never ever feel ashamed to start over again once you realize you've been doing something wrong. And always, *always* be willing to say, sincerely, to anyone at any time, "I'm sorry" or "Forgive me" or "I was wrong."

But no, I haven't thrown out all those lofty goals I once made in youthful zeal. I've just built a lofty *ladder* to them instead.

And my five guidelines are amongst the many steps on my personal ladder—that, yes, leads to those often far-seeming "stars."

I also have an underlying motto that guides each step that I take on the ladder: *Don't focus on staying motivated. Focus on staying active.*

It is through staying *active* that we prosper. Because let's face it: Every time we wake up and see that it's time for prayer—whether for *Tahajjud* or *Fajr*—we're not always happy (or "motivated") to get out of bed and pray.

So I tell myself: *No problem. Just get up anyway.*

Or...

No problem, just give charity anyway
No problem, just say 'I'm sorry' anyway
No problem, just [do that good deed, whatever it is] anyway...
And Allah will take care of the rest.

And maybe, just maybe, because of that single good deed you did that day, you'll be one of the beloved friends of the Prophet, *sallallaahu'alayhi wa sallam*, in the Hereafter.

Original version published via muslimahsource.org

9

I'm Muslim and Don't Pray, What Should I Do?

◆

I think most of us know how it feels to struggle in our faith. We know from personal experience the ups and downs in spirituality, so it comes as no surprise that a characteristic of *emaan* itself is that it increases and decreases. But the problem is, for many of us, our faith decreases more than it increases. Or more precisely, it keeps plummeting, and we feel powerless to stop it. For many of us, this problem has reached the point that our daily prayers are suffering. So we rarely pray with concentration, we rarely pray on time, and we often miss prayers.

Or we no longer pray at all.

What's the Solution?

Most likely, you'll hear a lot of conflicting advice on what to do if you're Muslim and no longer praying—some Muslims going as far as to tell you to not pray until you've worked on "more important things" first. But the reality is that, when it comes to one who has abandoned the prayer, there's nothing more crucial than reestablishing the prayer itself.

The only exception to this is regarding the one who has abandoned the prayer due to *shirk* (associating partners with Allah) or *kufr* (disbelief in Islam). Naturally, if a person is worshipping other than Allah or disbelieves in Him or any other article of faith (His angels, His books, His messengers, the Last Day, or predestination), then there is no benefit to reestablishing the second pillar of Islam (prayer) until the first pillar (belief) is once again in place.

However, for Muslims who still believe in the fundamentals of Islam, then there's absolutely nothing to work on before praying again—except to start praying again.

Nevertheless, as you resume your prayers, you definitely must address what led you to abandon the prayer in the first place. This requires spending time in sincere *du'aa* through supplicating to Allah and asking Him to help you overcome this spiritual trial. It requires engaging in honest self-reflection such that you identify those aspects of your lifestyle (and mindset) that are pulling you away from Allah. It requires reacquainting yourself with the fundamentals of *Tawheed* (the Oneness of Allah). It requires reflecting on the magnificence and greatness of Allah and learning His beautiful names. It requires setting aside time—alone—to reinvigorate your heart with heartfelt *dhikr* (remembrance of Allah). It requires reading and reflecting on the Qur'an such that Allah's words become divine guidance with practical implications specific to your life. It requires educating (and reeducating) yourself about your purpose in life and the reality of your affair in the Hereafter.

And it also requires taking an honest, objective assessment of from where and from whom you are learning your faith and of what you are being taught about Allah's religion. Because sometimes our spiritual crisis is a sign that we are in the wrong crowd, literally.

But regardless of the source of your spiritual crisis, if you've abandoned the prayer, then your first priority must be to reestablish it again.

What's the Point?

"I stopped praying because, I mean, what's the point?" someone said to me. "I wasn't getting anything out of it."

This was the first time that I realized that some Muslims see the benefit and purpose of prayer as rooted in human feeling. *Have we strayed so far that we no longer believe in the Unseen?* I asked myself. *Do we really imagine that we can determine spiritual reality based on human perception? And if you're Muslim, is it even* possible *to get absolutely nothing out of prayer?* I wondered.

The truth is this: If the only thing we gain from standing in prayer is that the angels have recorded that we stood in prayer, then that's *something*. And no matter how "pointless" you imagine those perfunctory movements to be, they are quite monumental to Allah—even if you're not always focused or in a state of concentration during prayer. Allah says,

> *"Never will I allow to be lost the [good] work of any among you..."*
> —*Ali'Imraan* (3:195)

And what good work is more important than doing what is minimally required in worshiping your Creator?

Prayer Is the Point

All good deeds are not equal, and when it comes to our faith, the importance of prayer cannot be overemphasized. After declaring the Oneness of Allah and His sole right to worship, prayer is the single most important act of a Muslim. However, prayer is not only the second pillar of the Islamic faith, it is also the second pillar of *your* faith.

In other words, unlike the vast majority of good deeds (i.e. wearing hijab, not drinking alcohol, or avoiding adultery and fornication) without prayer, you are treading the path to *kufr*—leaving Allah's religion.

Allah says,

"And they were not commanded except to worship Allah, [being] sincere to Him in religion, and to establish Salaah *[five daily prayers], and to give* zakaah *[obligatory charity]. And that is the correct religion."*
—*Al-Bayyinah* (98:5)

Prophet Muhammad (peace be upon him said), "Islam is built on five [pillars], testifying that nothing has the right to be worshipped except Allah alone and that Muhammad is the Messenger of Allah, performing the [five daily] prayers, paying the *zakaah*, making the pilgrimage to the House, and fasting in Ramadan" (Bukhari and Muslim).

Just as a physical structure cannot stand without its foundational pillars, your Islamic faith cannot stand without the foundational pillar of *Salaah*. Prophet Muhammad (peace be upon him) said, "Between us [the believers] and them [the disbelievers] is the prayer, and whoever leaves it falls into *kufr*" (Al-Tirmidhi, *saheeh*). The Prophet also said, "What is between a person and committing *shirk* (associating partners with Allah) and *kufr* (disbelief) is abandoning the prayer" (Sahih Muslim). He said further, "The first matter that the servant [of Allah] will be brought to account for on the Day of Judgment is the prayer. If it is sound, then the rest of his deeds will be sound. And if it is bad, then the rest of his deeds will be bad" (Al-Tabarani; *saheeh*, Sahih al-Jami).

Thus, establishing prayer *is* the point.

Shouldn't I Work On My Heart First?

One of the most widely spread—and spiritually destructive—myths amongst Muslims today is the idea that we should purify our hearts *before* reestablishing the prayer or doing any good deed. Some Muslims go as far as to say that the only spiritual motivation for prayer is love of Allah; thus (they say), if our hearts are not filled with love of Allah, then we shouldn't pray until it is.

However, our Creator tells us that submission comes before even *emaan* (true faith) itself; and certainly, it is impossible—logically or spiritually—to have a heart filled with love of Allah unless it first has true *emaan*.

Allah says,

"The bedouins say, 'We have believed.' Say [to them], 'You have not [yet] believed; but say [instead], "We have submitted," for faith has not yet entered your hearts.' And if you obey Allah and His Messenger, He will not deprive you from your deeds of anything. Indeed, Allah is Forgiving and Merciful."
—*Al-Hujuraat* (49:14)

Thus, a Muslim can never know, let alone declare, that true faith has entered his or her heart. The most we can hope for as Muslims is that, through our submission and obedience to His commands, Allah will love us, forgive us, and have mercy on us—in this life and in the Hereafter. But the only way to attain this love is through fulfilling our religious obligations, the first of which is establishing the prayer. This method (and only this method) is the means of drawing closer to Allah.

In a famous Qudsi hadith, the Prophet (peace be upon him) said that Allah says, "My servant draws not near to Me with anything more loved by Me than the [obligatory] religious duties I have enjoined upon him, and My servant continues to draw near to Me with supererogatory works so that I shall love him..." (Bukhari).

"Work on Your Heart" Myth

Recently, Saudi Beauty Blog posted a moving piece entitled "Are You a Muslim Who Doesn't Pray? Read On" (http://saudibeautyblog.com/are-you-a-muslim-who-doesnt-pray-read-on/) by an author who ascribes to the "work on your heart first" myth. The author says,

"The problem with most advice on salah is that it looks at things from a reactive point of view instead of a proactive point of view. Not praying? Well, just start. Or better yet, take one salah at a time and keep building until you reach five. Good advice, no? No. It doesn't address what leads a person towards salah to begin with...We pray because of one simple reason: We love Allah."

The author goes on to tell us what we should do instead of prayer so that we can put this love of Allah in our hearts: *"I always tell people who aren't praying to begin first with dhikr. Say SubhanAllah 100 times each day."*

From a literal standpoint, it is unclear how saying specific *dhikr* as a response to abandoning the prayer is any less reactive—or any more proactive—than saying prayer in response to abandoning the prayer. Both the recitation of *dhikr* and the reestablishment of prayer are responses (i.e. reactions) to the crisis at hand, yet both offer something proactive (i.e. doing an actual good deed) as a solution. But what *is* clear is the major difference between the reactive/proactive deed of *dhikr* and the reactive/proactive deed of prayer: Only the reestablishment of prayer actually addresses *and* solves the problem at hand.

However, it remains unclear why an optional deed should ever take precedence over an obligatory deed, especially given that our Creator tells us the exact opposite: *"My servant draws not near to Me with anything more loved by Me than the [obligatory] religious duties I have enjoined upon him...".* But the author assures us that inversing the order of Allah's commands will give us the same result. She says, *"You're not praying (yet) but be mindful that you are getting closer."*

But aren't you also getting closer to death? I thought to myself. And what if you die during this pre-prayer *dhikr* stage? Is this really okay?

After sharing a series of moving stories from the past, inspirational hadith, and heart-touching quotes, the author assures us that this is definitely okay. She says,

"So begin by walking towards Him. And be mindful that when you do your dhikr, you are taking a step. Another good step is to begin learning His Names. When you KNOW Him, really know Him, you can't help but attach your heart onto Him. Knowing Allah's Names will draw your heart closer to Him. And as it does so, you will remember Him more... Over time, your desire to please Him and turn back to Him will increase.. And this, my friends, is what will fill you up. This is what will take away the hollowness.. THIS is what will make salah easy. THIS is where the advice, 'take it one salah at a time' will be beneficial. When you get to this place, it won't be such a giant leap to contemplate standing up for one prayer. And slowly, one will become two.. And so on."

When I read this, I was moved by the power and truth of these words because reciting *dhikr*, getting to know Allah, and learning about Allah and His beautiful names will certainly assist us in removing the emptiness and hollowness we often feel in prayer (and at other times). However, again, I couldn't understand why the one act that brings together all of these things (*Salaah,* prayer itself)—and represents the most basic and most proactive form of *dhikr* and getting to know Allah—

should be put on hold in an effort to engage in the very things that prayer establishes for us.

But the author says that *"before you begin building your prayers, take the time to build your foundations, just as the early Muslims did. Start with baby steps, like doing dhikr or learning His Names."*

She also says, *"Allow yourself to be in a state where you know you aren't doing what you're supposed to, but you're taking steps to get there. One of the tactics of Shaitan [Satan] is that he leads you to believe that it's all or nothing. Either you're praying, or you're sinfully not. So when we're not, a dark cloud of guilt hovers over us, leaving us in darkness, unable to move forward."*

Myth vs. Truth

The "work on your heart first" myth is rooted in several erroneous beliefs about *emaan* (Islamic faith) and numerous misunderstandings of the prophetic message and Islamic history. Below is a list of some of the more serious errors and misunderstandings connected to this myth, followed by the correct Islamic point of view:

Myth: The good condition of the heart (*emaan*) is separate from the performance of obligatory deeds (hence the requirement to fill the heart with love of Allah before praying).

Truth: In Islam, the good condition of the heart is *dependent upon* the performance of obligatory deeds. In other words, your heart will <u>never</u> be filled with love of Allah (as defined by Allah) except *after* or *during* doing what He has commanded.

Myth: Purification of the heart is a static, sustained reality (hence, again, the requirement to have a pure heart before praying or doing other good deeds).

Truth: Purification of the heart is an ever-changing, action-based struggle that forms the very essence of *jihaad al-nafs* (the soul's ongoing battle against the self for the purpose of obeying Allah). Just as the physical purification of the body requires daily cleansing and consistent good hygiene; the spiritual purification of the soul requires daily prayer and consistent good deeds. Thus, it is impossible for your heart to be in the static state of sustained purification such that you can now move on to something else. This is because your heart is *always* in need of purification, so you can <u>never</u> move on to something else. In fact, why would you need to when that "something else" (i.e. prayer) is purification itself?

Myth: The human being has accurate, measurable knowledge of the spiritual state of his or her own heart (hence the alleged ability to know when your heart is spiritually pure or full of Allah's love enough to start praying).

Truth: Only Allah knows the state of our hearts, so we can <u>never</u> declare that we know or love Allah on any meaningful level except to the extent that we know we are Muslims and not disbelievers. However, Allah does give us signs regarding the state of our hearts, but those signs are primarily external rather than internal. In other words, the closest we can get to having an accurate *idea* of what is going on in our hearts is through looking at how we live our lives, especially regarding our religious obligations.

But even then, **the only spiritual state that we can conclude with any level of certainty is our heart's spiritual corruption, not its purity.** For example, if we believe in Allah and know how to pray, yet we are not fulfilling this basic Islamic obligation, then we can be almost 100% sure that our heart is in one of the most spiritually corrupt, diseased states possible—even if we are engaging in *dhikr*, reflecting on Allah and His names, and taking the other "baby steps" the author listed in her article. However, if we are praying all our prayers, and to the best of our knowledge and ability, we are fulfilling every religious obligation Allah has required for us, then we can *hope* that our heart is in a state of spiritual purity and love of Allah, but we must bear in mind that these good deeds might be rooted in arrogance (the belief that we are better than other Muslims) or *riyaa* (doing good deeds for a purpose other than pleasing Allah).

Myth: Except for the first pillar of Islam (testifying to the Oneness of Allah), the pillars of Islam are not foundational to a Muslim's *emaan*, (hence the advice, "*before you begin building your prayers, take the time to build your foundations*").

Truth: The five pillars of Islam are not only foundational to your *emaan*; along with the six articles of faith, they form the very essence of your *emaan*. Without them, you have no faith. This is because in Islam, *emaan* is both belief <u>and</u> action. Although some obligatory deeds are not foundational to our faith (i.e. wearing hijab, not drinking alcohol, or avoiding adultery and fornication), the five pillars of Islam most certainly are. In fact, the very meaning of the Arabic term *arkaan* (pillars) indicates something that is so foundational that, without it, whatever is built will collapse and be of no use or benefit.

Myth: It is obligatory to know and declare (to yourself) the pure state of your heart (hence the requirement to fill your heart with Allah's love before praying, thus necessitating both knowledge and declaration of spiritual purity).

Truth: It goes against the guidance of Allah to express knowledge of the Unseen or to ascribe purity to yourself. Allah says, *"...So ascribe not purity to yourselves. He knows best him who fears Allah and keeps his duty to Him"* (*Al-Najm*, 53:32).

Myth: Intentionally disobeying Allah is an acceptable path to ultimately obeying Him and drawing closer to Him (hence the instruction to continuously abandon the prayer as you takes "steps" to pray one day).

Truth: Obeying Allah and constantly repenting for our sins is the only acceptable path to obeying Allah and drawing closer to Him. **Just as *shirk* can never be an acceptable path to *Tawheed* or worshiping Allah alone, disobeying Allah can never be an acceptable path to drawing closer to religious obedience.**

In Islam, the path to worshiping Allah is worshiping Allah. The path to obeying Allah is obeying Allah. The path to *Tawheed* is *Tawheed*. The path to following the Sunnah is following the Sunnah. Nevertheless, this does not negate the fact that a person might commit *shirk* then ultimately repent and live a life of *Tawheed* and worshiping Allah; and a person might consistently disobey Allah then ultimately repent and live a life striving upon obedience to Him. However, these are not human-initiated realties, they are Allah-initiated realities; and that is no small distinction. As a human being, you must focus on the only reality that Allah has asked you to initiate: striving your level best to worship and obey Him at all times, most especially regarding the foundations of your faith, of which *Salaah* is one.

Myth: You can sin without being guilty of sin (hence: *"One of the tactics of Shaitan [Satan] is that he leads you to believe that it's all or nothing. Either you're praying, or you're sinfully not"*).

Truth: Sin is sin, so if you are knowingly not doing what you were commanded to do, then you are in sin. Unless you have a circumstance in which you are no longer held accountable for your deeds (i.e. total loss of your mental health or full possession by jinn), then there is no way to abandon prayer and not do it "sinfully." However, Allah is All-Forgiving and Merciful to believers who turn to Him in repentance; but in order to repent, we must first recognize that we are in sin in the first place, and then *leave* the sin (i.e. return to prayer) in order for our repentance to be accepted.

But it is true that one of the tactics of Satan is leading you to believe that it's all or nothing—and this is precisely why it is important to always pray, even when you feel hollow or empty inside. It's okay if you don't feel the love of Allah in your heart during *Salaah*. It's okay to work on building your love and knowledge of Allah *as you continue to pray*. In fact, in Islam, this is the only correct way to address this spiritual crisis.

However, Shaytaan [Satan] will lead you to believe that the best remedy for your hollowness and emptiness during prayer is to continue to not pray. He'll lead you to believe that it's okay to allow yourself to be in a state of continual disobedience as long as you are "taking steps" to fix problem.

And while it's true that we must be patient with ourselves as we work to fix our spiritual deficiencies (i.e. We must continue to pray as we work on addressing the hollowness and emptiness we feel during worship), Shaytaan will have us believe that fixing the problem involves a method that, quite literally, turns Allah's instruction on its head: optional before obligatory vs. obligatory before optional (or vs. obligatory *and* optional). Meanwhile, Shaytaan keeps encouraging you in this "taking steps" stage as he eagerly awaits Allah seizing your soul while you are in a state of major sin (and perhaps disbelief).

Myth: But this is the same step-by-step method used by Allah and His Messenger during the early stages of his prophetic mission. Rules and regulations like prayer and hijab were mandated much later.

Truth: No, this is not the same method. **Under no circumstance—in the early or late stages of the prophetic mission—did Allah or His Messenger permit or condone intentional disobedience of Allah**, let alone the continuous abandonment of a foundational pillar of Islam for the purpose of instilling in the early Muslims' hearts knowledge and love of Allah. In fact, formal prayer was one of the first "rules" established during this "instilling in their hearts knowledge and love of Allah" stage of the prophetic mission; but it involved the night prayer, as the establishment of the five daily prayers came later (during *Israa'* and *Mi'raaj*).

However, it is true that most rules and regulations were revealed during the latter stages of the prophetic mission, but it is also true that whoever accepted Islam during this latter stage was expected and required to follow all of the rules and regulations of Islam revealed up to that point. Thus, the lesson we draw from the prophetic mission's step-by-step approach is that we must learn (and teach) Islam based on spiritual priorities—and without a doubt, the foundational issues of *Tawheed* and prayer must always be our highest and most urgent priorities.

Myth: Actions are by intention, so if I intend to pray one day then Allah will record that for me.

Truth: Actions are by intention, so if you know you are supposed to pray and you intentionally <u>don't</u> pray, then Allah has recorded that for you.

FINAL NOTES: You Won't Always Want What Is Good For You

Allah says,

> *"But as for him who feared standing before his Lord, and restrained himself from impure, evil desires or unlawful inclinations, then Paradise will be his abode."*
> *—Al-Naazi'aat (79:40-41)*

It is true that a good deed is only counted as a good deed if it is done for the sake of Allah, but it is <u>not</u> true that a good deed can't be for the sake of Allah if you don't want to do it in the first place. In fact, one of the distinguishing traits of the people of Paradise, as we see in the above *ayah*, is their tendency to do good deeds *even though their hearts are inclined toward something else.*

Yes, we should love praying. Yes, we should derive joy, peace, and satisfaction from prayer. And, yes, we should want to pray. But the reality of the human condition is that, more often than not, what *should be* and what *is* are two very different things. This why **the greatest gift that Allah gives believers is His mercy and forgiveness**, despite how we continuously transgress against our souls through continuously falling into sin.

Allah says,

> *"Say, 'O My servants who have transgressed against their souls, do not despair of the mercy of Allah. Indeed, Allah forgives all sins. Indeed, it is He who is the Forgiving, the Merciful."*
> *—Al-Zumar (39:53)*

But don't let Shaytaan rob you of this magnificent opportunity for Allah's mercy and forgiveness by leading you to believe that a foundational pillar of your faith (i.e. prayer) can be abandoned, even if only short-term, as a path of obedience and drawing closer to Allah.

10

Be Careful What You Feed Your Soul

◆

Most of us understand the psychological and emotional harm that comes from constantly exposing ourselves to negative, toxic social and personal environments. So we limit interactions with negative people, and we end toxic relationships. But when it comes to religion, we say things like, "If you truly have faith, nothing can shake it."

There was a time when I myself believed this and proclaimed the same. But today when I hear statements that attest to the unshakeable nature of "true faith," what comes to mind is the popular saying, "Fools rush where wise men wouldn't dare to tread."

Even the Prophet (peace be upon him) prayed, "O You who turns hearts, make my heart firm upon Your religion." (Tirmidhi, saheeh by Al-Albaani). In the Qur'an, Allah describes the believers as those who pray, *"Our Lord, let not our hearts deviate after You have guided us; and grant us from Yourself mercy. Indeed You are the Bestower"* (Ali'Imraan, 3:8).

Also, the Prophet repeatedly warned us about the dangers of bad companionship, and in the Qur'an Allah narrates the story of a person in Paradise reflecting on his time in this world and recalls a friend who would cast doubt on the truth of the Resurrection:

> *"...I had a companion [on earth], who would say, 'Are you indeed of those who believe, that when we have died and become dust and bones, we will indeed be recompensed?' He will say, 'Would you [care to] look?' And he will look and see him in the midst of the Hellfire. He will say, 'By Allah, you almost ruined me! If [it were] not for the favor of my Lord, I would have been of those brought in [to Hell].'"*
> —*As-Saffaat* (37:51-57)

And bad companionship does not come only in the form of friendships. It also comes in the form of our social, academic, and work environments. It can also come in the form of what we expose ourselves to through the media, whether for entertainment or listening to "the news."

Naturally, because we live in this earthly world, we interact with friends and neighbors, we go to school and work, and we remain abreast of what is happening around us. However, if we hope for both good in this world and good in the Hereafter, we cannot afford to be only active participants in our worldly pursuits. We must also be active participants in our spiritual pursuits.

In the Qur'an, Allah says,

"And among the people is he who says, 'Our Lord, give us in this world,' and he will have, in the Hereafter, no share. But among them is he who says, 'Our Lord, give us the best in this world and the best in the Hereafter, and protect us from the punishment of the Fire.'"
—*Al-Baqarah* (2:200-201)

And we gain the best in both worlds, as well as protection from the Fire, by nourishing our hearts and souls with constant remembrance of Allah, prioritizing the five daily prayers, and working everyday to protect ourselves from spiritual degeneration—and by being ever aware of the human weakness in ourselves.

Perhaps it's okay to believe things like, *If you truly have faith, nothing can shake it*—so long as you recognize that true faith does not come from you. It is a gift from Allah. We just need to make sure that our hearts are ready to receive this gift...

By protecting ourselves from toxic relationships and environments that prevent our hearts from being open to Allah's guidance.

So be careful what you feel your soul.

11

Is It a Test or a Punishment?

◆

"How do I know if it's a test or a punishment?" This is a question I wondered about for years, and every chance I got, I asked an Islamic teacher or read whatever I could on the issue. Till today, the answer that stays with me is this: You don't.

Ultimately, only Allah knows why He's putting believers through certain trials. Also, a test and a punishment are not mutually exclusive. Both could be happening at once.

All of life is a test for the human being, so everything we experience is meant to direct us back to our purpose: worshipping and serving our Creator. Whether we are experiencing ease or hardship, enjoying the worldly fruit of honest hard work, or suffering the bitter consequences of arrogantly disobeying Allah; we have in each circumstance the opportunity to seek Allah's pleasure, beg His forgiveness, and attain Paradise when we die.

In other words, even if the worst is true—we're being punished for our sins—this in itself isn't "the end of the world." Often, believers experience pain, trials, and punishment on earth so that they are spared from torment for their sins in the Hereafter.

And if the worldly trial—or punishment—is encouraging us to turn to Allah, repent, and improve our spiritual lives; what practical benefit do we gain from obsessing over whether or not Allah is angry with us?

Unless we are arrogantly seeking to continue disobeying Allah and need a serious reality check, fixating on this question can become a distraction from spiritual growth itself. No matter what is or is not happening in our life (and why), we should be worshipping Allah and seeking His guidance and forgiveness anyway.

And would—or should—knowing whether you are facing a trial or a punishment change this noble focus for you?'

12

It's About What Your Heart Wants Most

◆

In the end, everything boils down to what your heart covets most. Worldly circumstances and experiences only bring to surface who you already are deep inside. This is why relatively identical trials—whether of prosperity or adversity—bring out the good in some and the evil in others...and why some of us become more humble with time and why some of us become more arrogant.

Yes, we all have very rational reasons for why we view ourselves and the world through a certain lens, but rarely do we ponder the deeper reasons for our conclusions.

The truth is, when it comes to our spiritual outlook—whether we believe adhering to God's laws leads to the solution or to further problems upon earth—our conclusion has more to do with our hearts than with any "proven" worldly reality.

The humble heart has faith in God's wisdom and guidance, fully aware that it doesn't have the capacity to effect ultimate good or bad upon earth, while the arrogant heart actually believes it can not only effect ultimate good or bad upon earth, but that it also has the capacity to accurately analyze and measure the root of all righteousness and evil in this world.

The irony is, in the end, the earth will never see "ultimate good" no matter what worldly system you value, religious or secular. So whether we ascribe to God's laws or to secular legislation, evil will still remain—because the source of evil is in the human heart, not in any ostensible worldly system. And the system we prefer is ultimately due to the state of our hearts, not to the state of the world.

Humble people tend to have faith in God and what He decrees—because ultimately their hearts covet the everlasting good in the Hereafter, so it matters little what good or bad they experience on earth. And arrogant people tend to have faith in only what they and others humans decree—because their hearts covet the transient, fleeting good of this world, as they believe their entire purpose rests in the good or bad they experience on earth.

Yet, ironically, it is only the people who are humble believers in God who will taste both the good of this world and the good of the Hereafter—and who will effect the highest possible good on earth. Meanwhile, arrogant people (who will effect the worst possible evil on earth) will remain restless, bitter and discontent, no matter how much good they experience, because their arrogant hearts make them distrust the only One who can provide the worldly good they covet most.

13

Good Muslims Do Bad Things Too

♦

Inaya's Struggle

Inaya is sixteen years old. She's memorized Qur'an and is an inspiration to youth and adults alike. She's inspired other girls to wear hijab and respect the rules of Islam. She even teaches Qur'an to children on the weekend. But there's only one problem. When her mother isn't looking, she removes her hijab after leaving for school, and she hides her Islam from teachers and classmates…and she likes a non-Muslim boy.
In other words, Inaya is living a double life.

And to make matters worse, Inaya's mother, who converted to Islam when Inaya was a child, thinks the only real Muslims are those who favor women wearing all black and *niqaab* (the face veil). When Inaya's Arab stepfather asks Inaya's mother Veronica to consider making exceptions to covering her face in America, Veronica becomes indignant and vents to a friend. Incidentally, Inaya overhears part of the conversation after she returns home from school, where she'd secretly removed hijab for the first time:

"What about Inaya?" Veronica said, the question halting Inaya's steps after Inaya closed the front door and stepped inside. "If I take off my face veil, how do I explain that to her?" Veronica groaned. "Next thing you know, he's going to ask me to start wearing colored hijabs." Silence followed for several seconds before Inaya heard her mother moan in exhaustion. "I know, *ukhti*," Veronica said. "I'm not saying it's *haraam*. I'm just scared he might ask me to take off hijab eventually."

Inaya dragged herself to the kitchen, sadness weighing on her.

"I'm not overreacting," Veronica said defensively. "Why should I uncover my face? Even if *niqaab*'s not obligatory, what's the point of taking it off? I fear Allah, not the people."

Inaya glanced at the clock. It was almost four o'clock, and she hadn't even prayed *Dhuhr*, the early afternoon prayer, and it was almost time for *Asr*.

"Because that stupid Arab culture made Sa'ad ashamed of his wife." Veronica's tone was indignant. "And now *I'm* supposed to feel ashamed for practicing the *Sunnah*?" She huffed. "They can keep their on-off hijab crap to themselves."

How Could You Portray a Good Muslim Like That?

The above excerpt and story line are taken from my novel *Muslim Girl*, and although the response to the book has been overwhelmingly positive, the story has received its share of criticism. How is possible that a Muslim author could take such a praiseworthy act like memorizing the Qur'an and associate it with a girl removing her hijab behind her parents' backs, hiding her Islam at school, and liking a non-Muslim boy?

Well, it's not the memorization of Qur'an that is being linked to Inaya removing her hijab and living a double life. It's her humanity. It's just that this particular human being happened to have also memorized Qur'an and is generally viewed as a "good Muslim" in the community. The point of this complex scenario is simply that our humanity and obligation to strive against our faults and sins does not magically disappear just because we happen to love reading Qur'an and inspiring others to do good.

But more than that, in my view, presenting real-life struggles—which often include pretty shameful behavior—demonstrates on a practical level why we do righteous acts like memorize Qur'an and wear hijab in the first place. We do not engage in righteous behavior because we are already pure. We engage in righteous behavior because we hope to be purified.

However, we live in a pretty confusing time, especially for Muslim youth, who are often thrust into contradictory environments simultaneously. On the one hand, their parents teach them to be good Muslims, have righteous companions, and put Allah first in everything. On the other hand, their parents leave Muslim lands and communities and enroll the youth in public schools and secular colleges, and they genuinely expect actions like wearing hijab and memorizing Qur'an to act as fool-proof shields against any human weakness and sin.

On top of that, even when these youth seek out Muslim company and environments, whether online or in their local communities, they find that the culture of "religious" Muslims is often cliquish, uppity, and hostile. The Muslims who consider themselves more knowledgeable than others feel free to dictate not only what "weak" Muslims *should* be doing, but also what "good" Muslims couldn't *possibly* be doing.

On the surface, it might appear as if these practices are aimed at simply commanding good and forbidding evil. But in practical reality, this is not what is happening. Many of these "religious" Muslims announce and publicize others' faults. Many storm social media sites and Facebook pages by posting Qur'anic verses, hadith, and threats of Hell Fire to "advise" those they disagree with—even regarding matters in which there are legitimate differing opinions. Many spend an inordinate amount of time obsessing over the "right" hijab such that even women who are already fully covered are subjected to constant criticism and harassment. And even when Muslims are doing nothing visibly wrong, these Muslims *dig* for evil to forbid. Then they openly question and reproach others for trivial decisions like having a profile picture or posting a status or link unrelated to the suffering in Palestine and Syria.

Why then does it come as a surprise that some youth who are genuinely striving to be good Muslims stay away from other Muslims, avoid Islamic activities, and minimize their trips to the masjid itself? For certainly, if those who are committing no clear sin are berated for being "bad Muslims" just because someone holds a different *fiqh* opinion than they do, where in the world do youth go who *are* committing clear sin and merely want a spiritually safe environment to get back on track?

What Is It That You Really Want?

In this suffocating environment, it often feels as if the decision to become visibly Muslim is simply a public announcement to other Muslims that they now have the right—and "Islamic obligation"— to make your life miserable until they appoint themselves as overseers of every detail of your life, from your decision to wear a certain scarf pin to your decision to pursue a certain career path or even marry (or not marry) a certain person.

What is it that you really want? I think this is a question that each of us must honestly ask ourselves. Do you want your brother and sister to live a life dedicated to pleasing and serving Allah? Or do you want them to live a life dedicated to pleasing and mimicking you?

This might sound like a rhetorical or even sarcastic question, but it really isn't. Most of us, myself included, would like to think that we genuinely want our brother or sister to dedicate his or her life to pleasing and serving Allah when we "advise" them on certain matters.

But what do our hearts and actions attest to?

This is a difficult question to answer, at least for those who truly wish to be honest with themselves. Many of us have enough Islamic knowledge and life experience to understand that, outside of adhering to foundational and clear, indisputable requirements in Islam, pleasing and serving Allah simply will not "look" the same for each individual Muslim. Why then do we keep perpetuating "Islamic" environments that are more focused on creating clones of ourselves than on fostering close relationships with Allah?

No, it isn't right for a girl to memorize and teach Qur'an then turn around and remove her hijab, hide her Islam, and try to hook up with a boy. But it also isn't right for us to tell Muslim girls and boys that they can't wear hijab or memorize Qur'an if they have these struggles or inclinations. Being human is a part of life. And our humanity doesn't disappear simply because we love doing righteous deeds.

Yes, we need to remind and advise each other toward good and away from sin. But we also need to understand that as we strive to do good and avoid sin, we should feel free to memorize Qur'an, wear hijab, and engage in any righteous action, even as we'll always have faults and sins to tend to. These righteous actions just might one day be the means through which we overcome the very faults and sins that people say a hijabi or memorizer of Qur'an couldn't possibly be doing.

And yes, we could even benefit from more *Muslim Girl*-type fiction stories in books. Because we have more than enough Muslim girl [and boy] true stories in real life. And given that so many Inayas of the world feel suffocated by modern "religious" culture, castigated by Islamic preaching, and unwelcomed in masjids, I think they at least deserve the opportunity to sit alone in their homes, open a book, and learn that yes, pleasing and serving Allah is possible after all—and that even if you're a "good Muslim," you'll sometimes do bad things.

And, even then, so long as you don't give up on your soul altogether, Paradise is for you too.

Originally published via muslimmatters.org

14
Judgment of Others Is Your Mirror

♦

"I don't care about yours or anyone's judgment of me," the woman shot back at me in an e-mail. I sat before the computer screen for some time, troubled by the words of someone I once knew as an intelligent, funny, and energetic person I enjoyed being around. I didn't know what to say in reply, or if there was anything I could say in reply.

I signed out of my e-mail and turned off my laptop, her words still on my mind…

Days before, I had been sitting in the library at work thumbing through a book when a line stuck out to me: *In the end, the kind of person you are is the result of what you've been thinking over the past twenty or thirty years* (Dr. Norman Vincent Peale, "Courtesy: Key to a Happier World").

I reflected on my own life thus far. *Who am I?* I thought. *What have I been thinking for the past twenty or thirty years?* I really didn't know.

I was reminded of a moment several years before, when I was invited to be part of a forum of five writers at a major Islamic conference in America. Each of us had been asked to give advice to aspiring writers in the audience. I remember sitting at a long table in front of the conference room in the company of an accomplished poet and songwriter, a nationally renowned journalist, and two other prominent authors. Because I had known in advance that I would speak and had to travel some distance to accept the invitation, I had carefully planned what I would say.

However, my carefully scripted speech was quickly discarded as I listened to the advice of some of my fellow panelists. One of the authors, the first to speak, drew on the advice of his spiritual mentor when he advised the audience to not be deterred by the "misguided" who believed in emulating the spiritual examples found in the Companions of the Prophet, *sallallaahu 'alayhi wa sallam*. The other author spoke of steering clear of stereotypical Muslim characters in his writing and described his ideal character as a Muslim woman punk rocker whose personal desires dabbed into those like the people to whom Allah sent the

Prophet Loot, *'alayhi salaam*. The journalist, a woman proud of her status as a non-practicing, non-hijabi Muslim, stood to share sentiments not too far from those of her predecessors, and it was her advice that troubled me most.

Today her precise words escape me, but the gist of them remain.

"I've been banned from speaking at masjids," she vented. "But I don't let that deter me. Never let others' judgment of you discourage you. Ignore what the people say about you, and keep doing what you believe in."

SubhaanAllaah, I remember thinking. Wonderful advice. Except there was one thing missing...

Years ago I remember reading for the first time the famous hadith of the Prophet, *sallallaahu 'alayhi wa sallam*, in which he taught that the believer is the mirror of the believer. Since then I'd reflected often on these words, and, honestly, I couldn't quite grasp what they meant.

Until I was looking in the mirror one day, as we often do when passing the glass reflection at home, and that's when it hit me.

In life, you never see your face. Ever. You learn how you look only through a physical reflection, a video camera or photograph—or through someone describing your face to you.

But never through your own eyes alone...

My name was called to the microphone and I walked to the podium, having only a vague idea of what I would say to the audience. I knew only that, whatever it was, it wasn't what I'd prepared beforehand. I took a deep breath, prayed silently to Allah and opened my speech with His Name. *Bismillaah...*

If I were to choose one word to describe what it means to write, I began, *I'd say "dangerous."* I paused, letting the word resonate in minds of the audience—and of my fellow panelists. *Dangerous, because once you've written something, it stays with you. In fact, it stays beyond you. It follows you to your grave. It lives on even as you don't.* I paused, hoping they were listening closely. *And every single word you've written, you'll answer for on the Day of Judgment.*

So my advice to aspiring writers is this: Be careful. Be very, very careful. And turn to Allah before you write anything. Ask Allah to guide your words so that they're pleasing to Him. And pray Istikhaarah before publishing anything.

Yes, others will judge you. It is true. And, no, we can't let others' judgment stop us from doing what we believe in. But this is only after you're sure, absolutely sure—beyond a shadow of a doubt—that what you're doing is correct—not according to what you think is right, but according to what Allah, our Creator, tells us is right.

For all those who wish to be successful writers, I advise you to pay attention to what others say about you. Pay very close attention. And yes, let it deter you. Let it stop you. Let it make you pause and think. And, yes, consider very carefully others' judgment of you before you move on.

Because it may be that in their judgment is the answer to your Istikhaarah.

After all, it is sometimes the case that people are opposing us because we need to be opposed...

I returned to my computer and signed into my e-mail account again, my mind now clear on why the woman's words had troubled me so.

I don't care about yours or anyone's judgment of me...

Her furious reply had been in response to a heart-felt e-mail I'd written to her because she had created a public persona that openly opposed Islamic etiquette and decency, and had several Websites soliciting support and sympathy from the world. I had ended my initial e-mail with a verse from the Qur'an about Allah's mercy and forgiveness:

"Say, O My slaves who have wronged their souls,
Despair not of the mercy of Allah.
Verily, Allah forgives all sins.
Truly, He is Oft-forgiving, Most Merciful" (39:53).

I don't care about yours or anyone's judgment of me, she had said to me in response. I thought of my impromptu speech at the Islamic conference, and I thought to myself, *But you should.*

I typed my final reply, carefully choosing the words I felt would be most effective in advising my struggling sister in Islam.

The believer is the mirror of the believer...

At that moment, I had a deeper understanding of the hadith. As believers, we need each other. Our believing brothers and sisters are the mirrors reflecting the countenance of our characters, and faith. Muslims, like all humans, are riddled with faults, contradictions, and faltering sense, so we need a mirror to be held in front of our faces—even when we wish to deny what's there—and even when we have crafted in our minds a completely different image than that which accurately describes us.

Without that mirror, we are prisoners—to our own faulty judgment, to our misguided determination, and to our errant thoughts and convictions.

In the end, the kind of person you are is the result of what you've been thinking over the past twenty or thirty years...

Yes, it is true, I thought—but only when it is only your own mind used as the mirror of your heart.

Originally published via saudilife.net

15

Yesterday, I Cried

◆

Author's Note: This blog was written when I lived in Riyadh, Saudi Arabia, and taught English at an international school.

It was one of those moments when you feel the tugging at your heart and the moisture behind your lids before you decide whether or not you want to...

The day started off as normally as one could hope. It was the weekend, a Friday, and I needed to run by a friend's house to pick up some books I needed for school.

Weekends are usually a stress relief for me, time to take a deep breath and exhale slowly. And I wouldn't have to hold my breath again until Saturday morning, when I'd return to work.

Before I go on, I think I should say that I'm a teacher—of high school girls. Anyone who's had the wondrous experience of working full time in a classroom full of "kids" knows the endless rewards of imparting knowledge on the next generation. And the endless heartache of having them impart stress on you.

I'm no exception.

So I was having one of "those days" (If you're a teacher, you know what I mean), when you wonder, *What's the point?* I mean, the world is going in a *drastically* different direction than I'd ever imagined. And the kids aren't too excited about an "old" woman standing in front of them, telling them that they should pray *Salaah* on time, wear hijab, and be "good Muslims."

Ho hum... Yes, I know. But what else can I tell them? "Which movie star couple do you think might accept Islam together"?

Anyway, I was stressed, to the point of heartache. I'd heard yet another story of a Muslim girl I'd once taught who was living a life wholly disconnected from Islam, and was sharing it with the world on Facebook. Sadly, today these stories seem endless. *Someone's at the mall meeting up with boys. Someone's throwing his number into cars. Someone's stopped saying their prayers...*

I arrived at my friend's house with a heavy heart, and was, as usual, wondering where my place was in all of this. After all, I have my own faults and my own soul to fend for. But still... There had to be *something* I could do. We're all in this together, right? We're here to help each other. You remind me; I remind you. That's what it means to be Muslim. At least that's what I'd been taught.

Who do you think you are? What gives you the right to tell others what to do? You need to mind your own business. You just think you're better than everyone else. You're so judgmental... These are just a few of the responses to seeking to help each other that believers hear each day. And it hurts. Oh, how it hurts.

I don't know about anyone else, but I find these words so painful because not only do I not think I'm better than others: I *know* I'm not better than others, yet I still have the obligation to command the good and forbid the evil. And that's no easy burden to bear.

In the end, I imagine that's why believers like the Companions, who were able to command the good and forbid the evil without ever giving up—even as they had faults of their own—are so highly praised in Islam. Allah says of them, *"You are the best people evolved for mankind. You command the good and forbid the evil, and believe in Allah"* (3:110).

I'm no scholar, but I find the wording of this verse quite compelling. Often, when Allah mentions the traits of the righteous, belief is mentioned before the performance of good deeds, as in the oft-repeated verses about *"those who believe and do righteous deeds."* But in this case, the good deed—commanding the good and forbidding the evil—is mentioned before even belief in Allah as the reason these believers are the best of all humankind. *SubhaanAllah.*

As I reflect on this, I take from it the lesson that true belief in not a private matter. It's not a personal spiritual state that only the person himself benefits from. Rather, it is a personal spiritual reality that is manifested outwardly, so much so that everyone who as much as crosses this believer's path benefits from him or her. This is what it means to have *eemaan*. This is what is means to believe in Allah.

These were the thoughts playing in the back of my mind when I, heavy-hearted, sat opposite my friend on her couch. The books I needed to borrow were stacked at my feet, and I was having a much-needed cup of tea. After that, I would return home to prepare for school the following week.

"I have to tell you something," my friend said in a hushed tone that let me know that whatever she was about to share was something she didn't want her children to hear. "It's about Barakah."

At her words, my heart grew heavier. Barakah was her eldest daughter and was fifteen years old. I told myself I could bear it, whatever it was. I sensed my friend wanted advice.

"But don't let her know I told you," she added. I nodded quietly, taking a sip of tea, wondering how my own daughter would be when she was Barakah's age. "She wouldn't like it if she knows I told anyone."

"I wouldn't do that," I said quietly, my mind distant, reflective.

This is the world we live in, I thought, pensive. *O Allah, help us, guide us, and give us strength,* I silently prayed. In that moment I thought of all that my friend had gone through the past year, deaths of loved ones, family friends leaving Islam, financial troubles... And now this.

Once, earlier in the year, as she lamented the loss of someone close to her, I said, "Remember, *ukhti*, when Allah loves someone, He tests them more than others." But right then, as I sat waiting to hear her struggles with Barakah, I didn't know what to say. So I remained silent and listened, my heart heavy from my own troubles, and hers.

"Barakah said she wants to memorize the Qur'an."

It took a moment for my friend's words to register and take meaning. My eyes widened slightly and my spirits lifted. "What?" I whispered.

A broad smile spread on my friend's face and tears gathered in her eyes. She nodded. "She told me yesterday. And she said, 'Ummi, you should too.'"

At that, my eyes filled, and I opened my mouth to reply, but I found no words. So I just let my heavy heart speak for me...

And I cried.

That was yesterday.

Today, I smile. And my eyes are still wet with tears. Because I know Allah is my Lord. He is *Ar-Rahmaan*—The Most Gracious. And there is, in believing in Him, always hope for the believer.

Original version published via saudilife.net

16

He Prayed In a Club!

◆

Somebody Should Slap Him?

It was a normal day at the college, and some of the Muslim students lounged in a break room after class. One of them had just shared the story of a Muslim boy who liked to party and often frequented clubs. "But when it's time for prayer," the student said, "he goes in the back of the club and finds a place to pray."

"What?" one Muslim girl proclaimed, her words laced in disgust. "Somebody should slap him!"

"Slap him?" her friend said, surprised. "Why would you slap someone for *praying*?"

"He's in a club!" the girl said, as if her friend hadn't understood the story herself. "How could he pray in a club?"

"Because he's Muslim and wants Allah to forgive him."

"Then he shouldn't be in the club in the first place!"

"But nobody's perfect," the friend said. "I'd want to encourage him instead of slap him."

"Encourage him? Are you serious? Then he'll get comfortable committing sin," the girl said. "No," she insisted. "I would slap him!"

"But prayer is the first thing we're asked about on the Day of Judgment," the friend said. "No matter what sins we're doing, we should never give up prayer."

"But in a *club*?" the girl said, eyes widened in disbelief. "He has no business praying in a club."

"At least he's praying."

"So you're willing to *encourage* him to pray in a club?" she said in shock.

"And *you're* willing to stop a Muslim from praying?" her friend retorted.

Bathing Is Only For Those Already Clean?

Prophet Muhammad, peace be upon him, said: "If there was a river at the door of anyone of you and he took a bath in it five times a day, would you notice any dirt on him?" They [the Companions] said, "Not a trace of dirt would be left." The Prophet then said, "That is the example of the five prayers with which Allah blots out evil deeds" (Bukhari).

Yet somehow in many religious circles today, we've come to believe that worship itself, as well as any place of worship, is only for those who are spiritually pure. Even if we ignore the fact that there exists not a single human being who is completely spiritually clean, this line of logic is counterintuitive and contradictory. It is like making a policy that bathhouses can only be used by those who are already clean.

Prayer Restrains Sin

It goes without saying that sin is evil and should be rooted out. And yes, we should speak against it or seek to remove it with our hands. However, let's not forget that before we are instructed to forbid evil, we are instructed to command the good. Thus, if someone is praying, our first priority should be to encourage this righteous deed. As for the evil this person does, the more we encourage them to pray, the less likely they are to continue in sin.

Allah says what has been translated to mean,

> "...And establish regular prayer. Verily, prayer restrains from shameful and evil deeds. And the remembrance of Allah is the greatest [thing in life] without doubt. And Allah knows the [deeds] that you do."
> —Al'Ankaboot (29:45)

So if you see someone committing evil, as we all fall into from time to time, share with them the greatest thing: the remembrance of Allah. And if you see them follow that evil up with a good deed like prayer, encourage them in the good instead of imagining that your personal disgust with their alleged hypocrisy is more important than their responsibility toward their Lord.

It's About Allah, Not You

Allah says,

> "Have you seen the one who prevents a slave when he prays?"
> —Al-'Alaq (96:9-10)

When you're feeling zealous of full of righteous indignation, a good rule of thumb to keep in mind is this: It's about Allah, not you. And if your heart should ever become so corrupted that you actually feel disgust at seeing a sinful person pray or perform any righteous deed, know that the problem is with you, not them. For indeed, preventing a servant of Allah from praying is more heinous than any sin that someone inflicts upon themselves.

Moreover, if you really believe that it is such a great evil for a person to follow up their sin with prayer, then tell me, O righteous one, what hope do you or any of us have in our affair in front of Allah?

Also By Umm Zakiyyah

If I Should Speak
A Voice
Footsteps
Realities of Submission
Hearts We Lost
The Friendship Promise
Muslim Girl
His Other Wife
UZ Short Story Collection
The Test Paper (a children's book)
Pain. From the Journal of Umm Zakiyyah
Broken yet Faithful. From the Journal of Umm Zakiyyah
Faith. From the Journal of Umm Zakiyyah
Let's Talk About Sex and Muslim Love
Reverencing the Wombs That Broke You: A Daughter of Rape and Abuse Inspires Healing and Healthy Family

Order information available at ummzakiyyah.com/store

Read more from Umm Zakiyyah at uzauthor.com

About the Author

Daughter of American converts to Islam, Umm Zakiyyah (also known by her birth name Ruby Moore), writes about the interfaith struggles of Muslims and Christians, and the intercultural, spiritual, and moral struggles of Muslims in America. Her work has earned praise from writers, professors, and filmmakers and has been translated into multiple languages.

To find out more about the author, visit ummzakiyyah.com or uzauthor.com, subscribe to her YouTube channel: uzreflections, follow her on Twitter and Instagram: uzauthor, or join her Facebook page at facebook.com/ummzakiyyahpage.

www.ingramcontent.com/pod-product-compliance
Lightning Source LLC
Chambersburg PA
CBHW051349040426
42453CB00007B/494